Introduction

What does clean really mean? A sparkling shine? A fresh scent? A squeaky feeling? Or is it about safety—removing contaminants that can cause illness? No matter what clean means to you, I'm sure you'd prefer the process to be free from harsh chemicals, excess effort, and high costs. That's where this book on DIY green cleaning recipes comes in!

Making cleaners, sanitizers, and soaps at home takes us back to a simpler time with less packaging, less effort, and fewer products. When a bit of alcohol, vinegar, water, plant-based soap, and herbs was all you needed to clean and sanitize your home and body.

The beauty of DIY cleaning products is that you know you aren't washing away grime with a long list of unrecognizable ingredients. Instead, you can choose your ingredients, customize the scents, and save money. The best part? These cleaning products couldn't be easier to make! In most cases, the recipes come together in mere minutes using common household ingredients that are easy to find.

In this book, I've created ten diverse recipes featuring common, natural ingredients, and then looked to the plant world to add therapeutic scents, skin-soothing properties, and natural cleansers. The first part is dedicated to digging deeper into the ingredients so you have a solid foundation before you start mixing. Armed with the recipes and knowledge of the ingredients, you can begin to customize the cleaners by using your preferred herbs and essential oils.

I hope this book launches you into the world of green cleaning with recipes that will keep your family safe, your skin healthy, and your home smelling like a garden!

LEISURE ARTS, INC. • Maumelle, Arkansas

Contents

12

16

24

All-Purpose
Cleaner
28

40

44

GETTING STARTED

Many natural ingredients have cleansing, disinfecting, antibacterial, or antifungal properties that make them ideal for DIY cleaning products. You may be familiar with some of these ingredients, while others may surprise you. Let's dig into the items you can use for cleaning and what makes them great cleansers and sanitizers. We'll also touch on the shelf life of your finished products and safety tips.

Ingredients

Bleach Alternatives

Bleach may be a popular ingredient in commercial sanitizers and cleaners, but it's highly toxic. It's an irritant to both the lungs and skin, making cleaning with it a hazard. The good news? Many other household cleaners are safe, effective, and easy to find that you can use instead of bleach.

Vinegar. Vinegar is acetic acid, which is effective at cleaning soap scum, grime, and stains. As long as it is diluted, vinegar can be used on multiple surfaces to disinfect and clean them safely. That being said, the same action that removes dirt and stains can dull the finish of shiny or porous materials like granite, some tiles, and hardwood. However, vinegar cleaner is a good option for tubs, toilets, kitchen appliances, and windows. There are many types of vinegar available in the grocery store from balsamic vinegar to apple cider vinegar. For cleaning, use the inexpensive white vinegar and save the other ones for your salad.

Baking soda. Baking soda or sodium bicarbonate is on the opposite side of the pH scale from vinegar. Its alkaline properties allow it to remove dirt and grease. It is also an excellent deodorizer. Baking soda absorbs aromas, so you can use it in the fridge, garbage can,

or litter box to eliminate unpleasant scents. To remove odors from carpets and upholstery, sprinkle on baking soda liberally and leave it overnight. In the morning, vacuum it up. Because baking soda is abrasive, you can mix it with water to form a paste that you can use to scrub away at tough dirt. Be careful not to scratch surfaces, though, and always do a small spot test before scrubbing a larger area.

Isopropyl alcohol. Isopropyl alcohol is sold as a mixture of isopropanol and water. It is labeled based on the amount of alcohol it contains, like 70% or 99.9%. This type of alcohol is readily absorbed into the skin and can be toxic at high doses. The purest form (99.9%) of isopropyl alcohol evaporates quickly and can be breathed into your lungs. When it is denatured with additives like water, the alcohol content is reduced to between 68% and 72%, and it is sold as rubbing alcohol. Rubbing alcohol is used as a medical antiseptic and industrial disinfectant and is generally considered safe for home use in small amounts.

Most natural cleaners and sanitizers can be made with ingredients that are safe for the skin and non-toxic. However, health authorities recommend a solution of at least 60% to 70% alcohol to kill viruses. If you want to make a sanitizer that will reduce your chances of catching viruses, it's necessary to include alcohol. All of the recipes in this book using isopropyl alcohol contain other ingredients to counteract some of its effects.

When using isopropyl alcohol in these recipes, it's important to do a spot check on your skin or the surface you're cleaning first and wait twenty-four hours for a reaction. Use these products in moderation, and be sure to get approval and advice from your health care professional. Be smart, be safe, and use them with care.

Vodka. Ethanol, found in grain alcohol or vodka, is a gentler alcohol disinfectant than isopropyl alcohol. Ethanol is a natural byproduct of plant fermentation, and the alcohol content varies. Vodka, for instance, is typically around 40% alcohol. At that concentration, it will not kill viruses, but it is still an exceptional disinfectant.

Hydrogen peroxide. Hydrogen peroxide is also a chemical compound that is usually diluted and sold as a mild antiseptic at around 3% concentration. Small amounts of it can be used as a surface cleaner or topically on wounds. However, it is not to be used on deep or severe wounds or burns.

Lemons, citrus, and citric acid. Lemons and other citrus fruits contain citric acid, which acts as vinegar does to clean. It is a mild antiseptic and antibacterial and also removes stains. Like vinegar, it can be tough on porous surfaces and finishes, so it is not recommended for hardwood, granite, or natural stone.

Lavender. *Lavandula angustifolia* is an herbal antiseptic and oil solvent that excels at cleansing and soothing the skin. Lavender's gentle fragrance is used in aromatherapy to promote calm, but it's cleaning power packs a punch! Adding lavender essential oil to recipes is beneficial for your skin and the surfaces you're cleaning. It's wonderful in the shower to prevent mildew and ideal in hand soap to speed skin repair. Add dried lavender buds to a muslin bag and toss it in your pillowcase, sock drawer, or dryer to add a fresh scent to linens. As a bonus, it can also be used as an insect repellant.

Tea tree. *Melaleuca alternifolia* oil is used as an antifungal and antiseptic skin treatment, but it is also used for cleaning and deodorizing around the house. A few drops of tea tree oil can be used when cleaning the toilet bowl, washing machine, coffee maker, and garbage disposal. It also works wonders on musty towels, dish rags, and pet bedding.

Castile soap. Castile soap is a specific olive oil soap that comes from Castile, Spain. For the recipes in this book, Castile soap refers to any plant-based liquid soap. It can be made from olive, coconut, avocado, or other plant oils. This biodegradable, non-toxic soap comes as a concentrate, so it should be diluted to the proper level according to the recipe. I always choose an unscented soap as my base and add my own essential oils.

Other Ingredients

Aloe. Aloe vera *(Aloe barbadensis)* is one of the oldest plants on record to be noted for healing properties. It has been cultivated worldwide due to its highly adaptable nature and usefulness as a skin-healing herb. Aloe is a natural antibacterial and contains antiseptics that help clean cuts and wounds. Aloe's pH level closely matches that of our skin, enabling it to gently (but thoroughly) cleanse skin while also closing the pores. Its anti-inflammatory qualities can calm inflamed skin. All of this makes aloe a fabulous ingredient in soaps and sanitizers.

Witch hazel. Witch hazel *(Hamamelis spp.)* earned its name because it was once popularly used for water witching, using a branch to locate water underground. Today, witch hazel is prized for its anti-inflammatory and skincare properties. A cotton bandage soaked in witch hazel can be frozen to create a cold compress for wounds and stitches. A spritz of witch hazel on your skin after a shower helps tone skin and reduce redness and inflammation.

Vegetable glycerin. After you use a bar of natural soap, you may feel like you didn't wash all of it off your skin. That silky coating left behind is glycerin. In commercial soap (which is technically not soap but a detergent), the glycerin is often removed and repackaged because it is more valuable on its own. Then, artificial moisturizers are added to the soap to replicate the glycerin's silky texture. Vegetable glycerin is made from plants like coconut, palm, and soy. When added to non-soap sanitizers, it can help protect and repair skin.

Essential oils. Essential oils are the concentrated herbal oils from a variety of plants. Claims that essential oils kill viruses and cure diseases are irresponsible and can be dangerous, but sadly, they are common. Think of these oils as a fine liqueur—just a few drops can add fragrance and herbal properties to home cleaning products. It's important to use essential oils with caution and in the way they are intended: in small amounts, heavily diluted, and never ingested. In this way, essential oils can add a lot of benefits to natural home cleaners, soaps, and sanitizers. But most of all, they'll make your recipes smell terrific and can offer you some aromatherapy as you use them.

Herbs. Fresh and dried herbs contain many cleansing and sanitizing properties. Because they are much less concentrated than essential oils, they are also much safer to use in recipes. Infusing vinegar with citrus rinds and fresh herbs is a wonderful way to add fragrance and herbal properties to a recipe, boosting its effectiveness and your enjoyment in using the finished product.

Shelf Life

In general, the expiry date of a product you make at home will be the earliest expiry date of the ingredients you use to make the recipe. For instance, if your recipes call for an ingredient that expires in six months and another that expires in one year, the final product will expire in six months.

That said, any ingredients that contain water are more susceptible to spoilage and microbial growth. Aloe vera, witch hazel, fresh herbs, citrus rinds, and any other organic ingredients will decrease the shelf life of your cleaning products.

Avoid contamination by sterilizing bottles, equipment, and surfaces before mixing your products, and always wash your hands thoroughly before and after mixing.

Each recipe lists its expected shelf life, but keep in mind that other factors, such as temperature, storage conditions, sanitation when preparing the recipes, and the quality of the ingredients, may impact shelf life. Your best bet is to make recipes in small batches and discard any that have taken on a different appearance, color, or smell since you created them. Store the finished products in a cool, dark space when not in use.

Safety

As with any product you use on your skin, it's important to know if you have any allergies or intolerances to the ingredients. The same is true for the surfaces in your home. Before the widespread use of any product, test it on a small area of your skin or home surface.

For skin, test the product on the inside of your elbow, and wait twenty-four hours to see if there is a reaction. For home surfaces, test the cleaner on a small, hidden spot. Wait twenty-four hours, then check to see if the cleaner caused any dulling or discoloration.

Above all else, use common sense and follow your health care professional's guidance for your individual health needs.

Basil & Bergamot-Scented Moisturizing Liquid Hand Soap

Makes 500 milliliters (approximately 2 cups) of soap

Whenever you find yourself washing your hands repeatedly, like during cold and flu season, it becomes increasingly important to add moisture back into the skin. Dry skin isn't just uncomfortable; it also breaks down the skin's protective barrier. As our skin breaks down, it is more prone to cuts, rashes, sores, and pulled cuticles, all of which provide entry points for germs. This liquid hand soap is made with gentle Castile soap along with moisturizing oil to help soften skin.

MATERIALS & INGREDIENTS

- 400 milliliters distilled or boiled water
- 100 milliliters unscented concentrated liquid Castile soap
- 1 tablespoon liquid oil (olive oil, almond oil, or avocado oil)
- 10 drops basil essential oil
- 10 drops bergamot essential oil
- Measuring cups
- Funnel
- 500-milliliter bottle with soap pump

Basil & Bergamot

Basil is often used on the skin to help repair balance and nourish it.

Bergamot is often used for its antibacterial and anti-inflammatory properties, which help to calm skin. It also adds a pleasant floral citrus scent to this liquid soap recipe.

Make It!

Step 1: Measure and combine the water and Castile soap.

Step 2: Add the liquid oil and essential oils.

Step 3: Use the funnel to pour the mixture into the bottle.

Step 4: Cap the bottle and shake well to combine.

HOW TO USE

Shake well before each use for the first few days. Over time, the ingredients will combine permanently, and shaking will not be necessary. Apply one or two pumps of soap to wet hands and lather for twenty seconds. Use a nail brush to remove any dirt hiding under your nails. Rinse well and dry with a clean towel.

Shelf life: This soap will last up to three months. Discard it if it becomes discolored or smells unpleasant.

Rosemary

Lime & Rosemary-Scented Foaming Hand Soap

Makes 400 milliliters of soap

Foaming hand soap feels luxurious on your skin. It comes out of the pump already lathered up, so it's silky and smooth. If you like a good bubbly lather, this foaming soap recipe is for you. As an added bonus, it has a fabulous bright lime and rosemary scent.

Foaming soap is 60% water, 20% prepared liquid soap, and 20% air. You can scale this recipe up or down based on this ratio to make as much or as little soap as you need.

While I love foaming hand soap, especially for use with children, keep in mind that working soap into a lather helps draw dirt from your skin into the bubbles, which are then washed away. Simply rubbing foam soap on your hands and then rinsing them immediately is not going to clean them as well as if you work the soap into a lather. Completely work the soap into your hands as if you're using liquid soap.

MATERIALS & INGREDIENTS

- 375 milliliters distilled or boiled water
- 25 milliliters unscented concentrated liquid Castile soap
- 20 drops lime essential oil
- 10 drops rosemary essential oil
- Measuring cups
- 500-milliliter Mason jar with foaming soap pump attachment

Rosemary & Lime

Rosemary is said to control oil production and has an antibacterial quality.

As a natural antioxidant, lime can help remove free radicals that damage cells, causing wrinkles, sunspots, and other and signs of aging.

Make It!

Step 1: Fill the Mason jar with the water.

Step 2: Add the Castile soap.

Step 3: Add the essential oils.

Step 4: Cap the jar and shake well to combine.

HOW TO USE

Shake well before each use for the first few days. Over time, the ingredients will combine permanently, and shaking will not be necessary. Apply one or two pumps of soap to wet hands and scrub for twenty seconds, working the soap over the front and back of your hands and between your fingers. When used this way, foaming soap is just as effective as liquid or bar soap.

Shelf life: This soap will last up to three months. Discard it if it becomes discolored or smells unpleasant.

Aloe & Witch Hazel Hand Sanitizer Gel

Makes 243 milliliters (approximately 1 cup) of sanitizer

In the past, I generally avoided hand sanitizers, preferring to wash my hands with soap and water to remove germs and viruses. However, sanitizer is great to have on hand when you're out and about.

Over the years, I've become somewhat of a hand sanitizer connoisseur, and you may be, too! You'll find that some feel slimy and others sticky, some have an overpowering fragrance, and others are terribly drying.

This hand sanitizer is designed to feel great on your skin, smell wonderful, and do an effective job of cleaning when soap and water are not available. It is not formulated to combat viruses. Instead, it simulates handwashing when there is no water and soap available (see the alcohol-based hand sanitizer recipe on page 20 for more information).

The ingredients are good for your skin, and the plants have beneficial properties for cleansing. By adding hand sanitizer to your personal cleaning routine in low-risk environments, your hands and skin will thank you.

MATERIALS & INGREDIENTS

- 80 milliliters pure witch hazel
- 160 milliliters 100% pure aloe vera gel
- 10 drops lavender essential oil
- 2.5 milliliters (½ teaspoon) vitamin E oil
- Measuring cups
- Small bowl
- Funnel
- Two 125-milliliter bottles with soap pumps

Make It!

Step 1: Mix the witch hazel and aloe vera gel together in a bowl.

Step 2: Add the essential oil and mix well. Then add the vitamin E oil and stir well to combine.

Step 3: Use the funnel to pour the mixture into the bottles.

Step 4: Cap the bottles and shake well to combine.

HOW TO USE

Massage a dollop of hand sanitizer into your skin, rubbing it all over your hands and between your fingers as if you were washing them with soap. Afterward, if available, use water to rinse your hands and dry them thoroughly.

Shelf life: Aloe gel hand sanitizer will last up to the expiry date of the aloe vera. This could be up to a year if stored properly in a cool location like the fridge. In the absence of expiry dates, or when using fresh aloe vera, discard aloe gel sanitizer after seven to ten days or sooner if it shows signs of spoilage.

Alcohol-Based Hand Sanitizer Spray

Makes about 200 milliliters of sanitizer

It only takes a few ingredients and just minutes to put together this alcohol-based hand sanitizer. This spray sanitizer can be used on both hands and surfaces in a pinch.

Public health officials recommend that hand sanitizer contain at least 60% alcohol to eliminate viruses, bacteria, and other germs. This recipe is more than 70% alcohol. It's not as moisturizing as the aloe hand sanitizer on page 16, but it is an alcohol-based option for when you need it.

Even though this alcohol-based recipe is harsher on the skin than the aloe version, I still prefer this homemade alcohol-based sanitizer over commercial options because the addition of glycerin and witch hazel does help soften skin. Plus, adding essential oils helps mitigate the strong smell of isopropyl alcohol. The alcohol aroma will dissipate quickly, but the scent of sweet orange and lavender will linger on your hands.

MATERIALS & INGREDIENTS

- 140 milliliters 99.9% isopropyl alcohol
- 25 milliliters vegetable glycerin
- 25 milliliters witch hazel
- 4 drops sweet orange essential oil
- 4 drops lavender essential oil
- 4 drops tea tree oil
- Measuring cups
- Funnel
- Two 100-milliliter spray bottles

Choose Soap & Water First

The best way to keep your hands clean is to wash them with soap and water regularly. Whenever washing is not possible, this hand sanitizer provides an alternative, portable option.

Make It!

Step 1: Add the glycerin and witch hazel to the alcohol.

Step 2: Add the essential oils.

Step 3: Use the funnel to pour the mixture into the bottles.

Step 4: Cap the bottles and shake well to combine.

HOW TO USE

Shake well before each use. Add a spray or two of sanitizer to your hands. Rub it all over your hands and between your fingers as if you were washing them with soap. Afterward, if available, use water to rinse your hands and apply moisturizer regularly.

Isopropyl alcohol is readily absorbed into the skin, so it's best to use it sparingly. In small amounts, there is not usually a negative reaction, but some skin may be more sensitive. Always do a small test first and watch for adverse reactions such as rash, redness, drying, or cracking skin.

Shelf life: The alcohol content in this recipe will prevent bacterial and mold growth. However, its potency will wane over time. Discard any unused sanitizer after one year to be safe.

Travel Disinfecting Wipes

Makes 30 wipes

Even though these disinfecting wipes are made with pretty cocktail napkins, don't let them fool you. They're still powerful enough to effectively clean your hands or surfaces.

Pack them with you when going to the grocery store to wipe down your cart or to wipe your hands before and after entering. They can also be kept by the door so you can wipe down your keys and phone each day when you arrive home. Keep them in a metal storage container and toss them in your bag so they're handy whenever you need them.

When you open the travel container, you will certainly be hit by the alcohol aroma. But once you rub a wipe on your hands, that will quickly dissipate, leaving behind the softness of coconut oil and the scent of lavender and lemon.

MATERIALS & INGREDIENTS

- Thirty 5" x 5" folded cocktail napkins
- 6" x 4" stainless steel food storage container with snap-on lid
- 350 milliliters 70% isopropyl alcohol (or dilute 99.9% isopropyl alcohol to 70% with distilled water)
- 15 milliliters (1 tablespoon) fractionated coconut oil
- 3 drops lavender essential oil
- 3 drops lemon essential oil
- Measuring cups

Fresh & Clean with Lemongrass & Pine

The combination of these two popular essential oil fragrances is one of my favorites for balancing. Calming, floral lavender and uplifting, bright lemon work together to leave a pleasant scent on your hands once the alcohol dissipates.

Make It!

Step 1: Fold all the napkins in half so they fit in the container.

Step 2: Mix the alcohol and coconut oil. Then add the essential oils.

Step 3: Place the folded napkins in the container and pour the mixture over them.

Step 4: With clean hands, press down on the napkins to ensure they're evenly saturated with the alcohol mixture. Close the container, add a label, and your wipes are ready to use.

HOW TO USE

Remove a wipe from the container and thoroughly rub it over your hands or the surface you want to clean. Discard the used wipe. Do not flush it or add it to green waste.

Shelf life: The alcohol content in this recipe will prevent bacterial and mold growth. However, its potency will wane over time, and the wipes will dry out. Keep the wipes in a sealed container to prolong their shelf life. Discard them when they have dried out or after one year to be safe.

All-Purpose
Cleaner

Orange & Sage All-Purpose Cleaner

Makes 1.5 liters of concentrated vinegar cleaner

The ingredients in this recipe could be used to dress a fresh salad, but they also have powerful cleaning properties!

Vinegar has been used throughout the ages for home cleaning because of its acidity. The acetic acid counteracts oil, soap, dirt, and sticky messes around the house. It also helps disinfect surfaces. The only thing I don't love about vinegar as a cleaner is that it doesn't smell that great. Combining orange peels and fresh garden sage with vinegar adds even more cleaning power and a beautiful fragrance that makes your house smell clean.

This cleaner is strong enough yet gentle enough to be used throughout the house, from kitchen counters to sticky stovetops, the bathroom, and even to mop the floors. The finished product is a concentrate that you can dilute based on the strength you need. Keep the concentration high for difficult cleaning projects and dilute it for light cleaning.

MATERIALS & INGREDIENTS

- 4–5 large oranges, peeled
- A handful of fresh sage leaves
- 1½ liters distilled white vinegar
- Sage essential oil (optional)
- Measuring cups
- Strainer
- 2-liter Mason jar with lid
- Spray bottle

Orange & Sage

Orange has a wonderfully uplifting scent that makes us feel cheery and bright. The orange oil found in the peels also has cleaning properties.

Sage is packed with antifungal and antibacterial properties. The ancient Greeks and Romans preserved meat with sage because of its ability to reduce bacteria. It makes a great addition to this all-purpose cleaner.

Make It!

Step 1: Add the orange peels and sage to the Mason jar.

Step 2: Top up the jar with the vinegar and keep it covered in a cool, dark place for one week.

Step 3: After a week, strain the liquid into another jar, bowl, or measuring cup.

Step 4: If you'd like a stronger herb smell, add a few drops of sage essential oil. Store the concentrate in a clean jar until you are ready to dilute it for use.

HOW TO USE

This homemade cleaner is all-purpose and perfect for bathrooms, kitchens, and floors.

Make a strong grease and soap scum cleaner for stovetops and bathrooms by combining one part vinegar concentrate with one part water In the spray bottle.

Make an all-purpose kitchen counter spray by combining one part vinegar concentrate with three parts water in the spray bottle.

Add ½ cup of vinegar concentrate to a gallon of warm water for mopping laminate and tile floors. For hardwood floors, don't use the vinegar concentrate. Instead, add a tablespoon of undiluted Castile soap to a gallon of warm water.

Shelf life: Use within six weeks. I recommend making small batches so you always have some fresh cleaner on hand.

alcohol
Cleaner

Lemongrass & Pine Alcohol-Based Disinfecting Kitchen Cleaner

Makes 880 milliliters of cleaner

Vinegar is a wonderful all-purpose cleaner, but not for granite or stone countertops. It's too acidic and will wear away the lovely finish of those surfaces, making them dull and lifeless. On the other hand, this alcohol-based cleaner is much gentler on your home surfaces but still tough on surface messes.

For this recipe, you can use any inexpensive, clear alcohol. I chose vodka and avoided the top-shelf brands. Vodka is only around 40% alcohol, which makes this recipe around 8% alcohol. This isn't sufficient to kill viruses but is good for disinfecting counters. If you'd like to increase the alcohol content of this recipe, use 99.9% isopropyl alcohol, which will bring the final product to 20% alcohol. If you want to sanitize a counter using at least 60% alcohol to address viruses, use the alcohol-based hand sanitizer or travel wipes instead.

MATERIALS & INGREDIENTS

- 700 milliliters (approximately 3 cups) water
- 175 milliliters clear alcohol (vodka or 99.9% isopropyl alcohol)
- 8 drops unscented concentrated liquid Castile soap
- 5 drops lemongrass essential oil
- 5 drops pine essential oil
- Measuring cups
- 1-liter spray bottle

Fresh & Clean with Lemongrass & Pine

Lemongrass essential oil is long-lasting with a strong scent. In some recipes, it can outshine and mask the other scents, which is exactly what makes it so appropriate in this recipe. Just a few drops give this cleaner the power to neutralize kitchen and bathroom smells. Pine is a disinfectant that leaves a fresh, clean scent behind and pairs well with the earthiness of lemongrass.

Make It!

Step 1: Measure the water and alcohol.

Step 2: Add the water, alcohol, and Castile soap to the spray bottle.

Step 3: Add the essential oils.

Step 4: Cap the bottle and shake well to combine.

HOW TO USE

Shake well before each use. Spray counters and wipe with a soft cloth.

Note: On stone counters, it's recommended to avoid using abrasive cleaners and tools like scrubby sponges, steel wool, and even baking soda. Granite can actually be scratched, so only use soft cloths and this alcohol cleaner recipe.

Shelf life: The alcohol content in this recipe will prevent bacterial and mold growth. However, its potency will wane over time. Discard any unused cleaner after one year to be safe.

Reusable Lemon & Rosemary-Scented Kitchen & Bathroom Wipes

Makes 16 reusable wipes

Use these reusable wipes to cut grease, grab grime, and remove soap scum with one fresh-smelling swipe of your hand. They look pretty enough to keep on the countertop where they're easy to grab for quick cleanups. The wipes are reusable, so toss them in the laundry when you're finished, and they'll be ready for the next round of cleaning!

MATERIALS & INGREDIENTS

- Two 30" x 30" muslin fabric squares
- 120 milliliters water
- 120 milliliters vinegar
- 10 milliliters (2 teaspoons) unscented concentrated liquid Castile soap
- 10 drops lemon essential oil
- [illegible] drops rosemary essential oil
- Measuring cups
- Scissors
- Large jar with lid

Lemon & Rosemary Forever

Lemon is the scent of clean. Its bright aroma does the job but doesn't linger too long, leaving behind only freshness. Rosemary is an excellent herb for deodorizing while adding an earthy, calming scent. Combined with lemon, it balances this recipe well for both kitchen and bathroom cleaning.

Make It!

Step 1: Take one of the muslin squares and fold it in half. Then fold it in half again lengthwise so you end up with a 30" x 7.5" rectangle.

Step 2: Cut the fabric at the folds to create four 30" x 7.5" strips.

Step 3: Fold each strip in half widthwise and cut at the fold to create eight 7.5" x 15" wipes.

Step 4: Repeat Steps 1 to 3 with the remaining muslin square to make eight more wipes. Place all sixteen wipes in the jar.

Step 5: Measure the water in a measuring cup. Add the Castile soap and gently stir to dissolve. Then add the vinegar and essential oils. (Note: Be sure to add the soap before the vinegar. Otherwise, it will clump and be difficult to dissolve.)

Step 6: Pour the mixture over the wipes. With clean hands, press down on the wipes to ensure they're evenly saturated with the mixture. Cover the jar with the lid.

HOW TO USE

Remove one wipe from the jar and use it to clean counters, sinks, and appliances. When finished, toss the wipe in the wash. Laundered wipes can be used again with fresh cleaning solution.

Shelf life: The wipes can be washed and reused repeatedly, but the cleaning solution should be replaced every three months. When removing wipes from the jar, be sure your hands are clean to avoid contamination and be careful to touch only one wipe.

Fruit & Vegetable Wash

*Makes 600 milliliters (approximately 2½ cups)
of fruit and vegetable wash*

A wash made of acid and salt makes it easy to remove some of the waxes, chemical sprays, and dirt that can stick to produce when it comes home from the grocery store. The ingredients in this fruit and vegetable wash help to get produce squeaky clean without adding an off-putting flavor.

Vegetables and fruit usually have some sort of microorganisms on them. In most cases, washing produce prolongs its life by removing these organisms. However, some fruit and vegetables have their own natural protective measures. For example, blueberries have bloom, a fine powdery covering that fights off the bacteria and fungus that would cause premature decay.

Most fruit and vegetables can be washed when they come home from the grocery store, but in some cases, you may want to wait to wash them until just before eating to prolong their shelf life.

MATERIALS & INGREDIENTS

- 475 milliliters warm water
- 120 milliliters white vinegar
- 2 tablespoons citric acid
- 2 tablespoons salt
- Measuring cups
- Spray bottle

Make It!

Step 1: Measure the warm water.

Step 2: Add the citric acid and salt and stir until both are fully dissolved.

Step 3: Pour the water mixture and vinegar into the spray bottle.

1

2

3

HOW TO USE

Spray produce to cover all surfaces, let it rest for two minutes, then rinse it off with tap water before consuming.

While this fruit and vegetable wash tastes rather good (if you like salt and vinegar flavored chips), it will not change or affect the flavor of the produce. As long as it's applied as directed, even soft-skinned fruit like strawberries and raspberries will not take on the salt and vinegar flavor.

Shelf life: Use this cleaner within three months and discard it if it changes color or has a strange aroma.

Tea Tree & Peppermint Toilet Bombs

Makes 16 to 20 ice cube-sized toilet bombs

If cleaning the toilet is not your favorite job, let these toilet bombs do the work for you! Keep a container of these fresh-scented cleaners in the bathroom, and pop one in the toilet when the bowl needs a refresh. They will fizz and bubble, releasing the cleaning ingredients and a fresh scent. They can also be used in sink drains and garbage disposals. Just pop one of these in the drain, and it will fizz away any grease, buildup, and stinky odors that may be lingering.

MATERIALS & INGREDIENTS

- 2 cups baking soda
- 1 cup citric acid
- 10 drops tea tree essential oil
- 10 drops peppermint essential oil
- 60 milliliters unscented concentrated liquid Castile soap
- 240 milliliters water
- Spray bottle
- Silicone ice cube mold (optional)
- Measuring cups
- Mixing bowl
- Spatula
- Parchment paper
- Jar with lid

Now That's Fresh!

Tea tree and peppermint are both superior at deodorizing. Tea tree has antifungal and antiseptic properties, and it's hard to beat the freshness that goes along with the scent of peppermint. This cheery combination will add some pep to the job of cleaning the toilet!

Make It!

Step 1: Add the baking soda and citric acid to a bowl and mix with a spatula. Add the essential oils and mix them in well.

Step 2: Combine the Castile soap and water in the spray bottle. Spray this solution lightly on top of the powder mixture, mixing it in quickly with your hands as you spritz. Continue to spray the powder and mix until it packs together easily in your hands like a snowball. Note: You will not need all the Castile soap and water mixture for this recipe. The amount varies and should be judged by how the mixture forms.

Step 3: Press the mixture into a silicone ice cube mold. If you don't have a mold, roll the mixture into balls about the size of ice cubes.

Step 4: Allow the mixture to set until firm and then pop the pieces out of the mold. Set the toilet bombs on parchment paper and allow them to dry until they feel firm. Store them in the jar.

HOW TO USE

Store toilet bombs in a jar and pop one out when you need to refresh your bathtub, sink, or toilet. Simply toss one into the toilet bowl and watch as it fizzes away, leaving the toilet clean and smelling fresh.

Use toilet bombs in the evening before going to bed for a fresh, clean bowl every morning. Or use them as needed between cleanings with an all-purpose cleaner.

Shelf life: These toilet bombs will last for years and still fizz as soon as they hit the water, but the essential oil fragrance will dissipate after a few months. Store them in a sealed jar to keep the scent from evaporating.

Stephanie Rose

Stephanie is an award-winning author, freelance writer, and instructor who aims to encourage healing and wellness through plants. She is trained as a Master Gardener, Permaculture Designer, Herbalist, and Natural Skincare Formulator. She is a member of Garden Communicators International, the Permaculture Institute of North America, and the International Herb Association and volunteers to develop children's gardens as a Master Gardener.

Stephanie has written several books, including *Garden Alchemy: 80 Recipes and Concoctions for Organic Fertilizers, Plant Elixirs, Potting Mixes, Pest Deterrents, and More* (Cool Springs Press, 2020), *Home Candle Making* (Leisure Arts, 2019), *Home Apothecary* (Leisure Arts, 2018), *The Natural Beauty Recipe Book* (Rose Garden Press, 2016), and *Garden Made: A Year of Seasonal Projects to Beautify Your Garden and Your Life* (Roost Books, 2015), which was a Gold Medal Winner from the 2016 Independent Publishers Book Awards (the IPPYs).

Stephanie lives in Vancouver, Canada, with her school-aged son and a cat named Magic. She can be found growing herbs in her urban garden or exploring beautiful British Columbia in her campervan. She shares stories, recipes, and projects on her inspiring website, *GardenTherapy.ca*.

Production Team: Designer - Michael Douglas; Graphic Artist - Michael Puckett; Editor - Katie Weeber.

Made in U.S.A.